WHISKEY BAKE

Baking with American Rye and Islay Scotch Whiskeys

Dedication

I dedicate Whiskey Bake to my parents in celebration of their 25th anniversary. Thank you Yabin for giving me courage in life. Thank you Richard for giving me the support I need in life. I want to thank you both for helping me make my dream of writing this book come true. I wish you happiness and health for decades to come!

WHISKEY BAKE
— *Baking with American Rye and Islay Scotch Whiskeys*
Jialin Tian, Ph.D.

Text and photographs copyright © 2019 by Jialin Tian

All rights reserved. No part of this book may be reproduced or transmitted in any form or by any means, electronic or mechanical, including photocopying, recording, or by any information storage and retrieval system, without permission in writing from the publisher.

Disclaimer: While every precaution has been taken in the preparation of this book, the publisher and author assume no responsibility for errors or omissions, or for damage or loss resulting directly or indirectly from the use of the information contained herein.

Published in the United States by
Jayca
2936 Burrows Ln
Ellicott City, MD 21043
USA

ISBN 978-1-7334779-0-1

First Edition 2019
www.macaronmagic.com

CONTENTS

INTRODUCTION **4**

BAKING COMPONENTS
Sea Salt Caramel **6**
Cranberry Jam **7**
Almond Paste **7**
Banana Mash **8**

AMERICAN RYE WHISKEY
Cranberry Macaroons **10**
Banana Cookies **12**
Banana Mash Dessert Glasses **14**
Breakfast Pancakes **16**
Banana Scones **18**
Banana Mini-Loaves **20**
Almond Bread Rolls **22**
Rustic Raisin Loaves **24**
Pumpkin Bread Rolls **26**
Puff Pastry Almond Tarts **28**
Bread Pudding **30**
Peach Custard Pie **32**
Cherry Cake Ring **34**

ISLAY SCOTCH WHISKY
Chocolate Peat **36**
Macaroons **38**
Double-Baked Cookies **40**
Cranberry-Almond Gems **42**
Rustic Shortbread **44**
Dessert Cake Spoons **46**
Almond Cakes **48**
Chocolate Cake Corks **50**
Islay Bread Rolls **52**
Islay Loaves **54**
Raspberry Cake Puddings **56**
Apple and Peach Pie **58**
Melon-Passionfruit Cake Ring **60**
Mango Loaf Cake **62**
BONUS COCKTAIL RECIPES 64

INTRODUCTION

I have been thinking of a new cookbook concept using spirits in baking for years. In July of 2019, after I returned from a trip to Scotland, I thought it would be interesting to combine my passion for baking and my love of whiskeys in one book. After all, the word whiskey is derived from the Gaelic expression "water of life." What could be more invigorating than bringing the water of life into baking and working the spirit of whiskey into bread? Baking with whiskey is easier said than done, however. As the alcohol evaporates so does some of the essence and aroma of the whiskey.

The making of whiskey involves a complex process. First, grains are made into mash, and the mash is then cooked to release enzymes that convert starches into sugars. This laborious process continues as yeast is added during fermentation to produce a distiller's beer. Whiskey comes to life when the beer is distilled into a spirit and matured in oak barrels for several years or decades. The flavor components of whiskey originate from the grains and the distillation process and are then enhanced by the interaction between the spirit and the barrels during maturation. The byproducts of the distillation and aging process are hundreds of aroma compounds that essentially set one whiskey apart from others.

To preserve the delicate flavors of whiskey in baking, I had to find a family of complementing ingredients that would not overpower the spirit. Almond flour, low in starch, high in protein, has a subtle sweet aroma and is an ideal mate for whiskey in baking. Wheat flour alone produces alcohol and carbon dioxide during natural fermentation. Unfortunately, this familiar process creates aroma compounds that can mask the whiskey flavors. By incorporating almond flour, we can achieve superior results while carefully balancing the ingredients. Cream cheese is another ingredient that works wonders with whiskey. The enzymes in cream cheese interact with the alcohol, which can improve the taste of and bring complexity to baked goods.

American rye whiskey originated in the Pennsylvania and Maryland regions during the colonial era. It was the first aged grain spirit European settlers made in America. Today, rye whiskey is experiencing a resurgence after playing only a minor role in the American spirit industry since Prohibition. Not surprisingly, rye whiskey is very easy to work with in baking; spices such as cinnamon, cloves, and toasted anise are typical foreground notes with the fruity and floral undertones found in American rye whiskey. This flavor profile works extremely well with bananas. In *Whiskey Bake*, I develop several recipes by using rye whiskey and fermented banana mash. The bread and pancakes baked with banana-rye whiskey mash are accented with hints of spices, and yet given much more depth thanks to the addition of rye whiskey. Another ingredient that boosts the personality of rye whiskey is almond paste. The light touch of bitter almond essence complements the sweet note in rye whiskey, which is well represented in a custardy sauce. Rye whiskey and fruits such as apples, peaches, and cherries are brilliant pairings as well.

For the longest time, I have been fond of Islay Scotch whisky; it is marked by its unique pungent peaty smokiness. Islay, an island sitting off the western coast of Scotland, is the home of a handful of distilleries that are known for producing the brawniest whiskeys in the world. While other whiskeys get their flavors from oak barrels, the signature aroma of Islay whisky was born from the fire and smoke of peat. When malted barley is embraced by peat smoke, the strong peat aroma is transferred to the whiskey. Peat, a source of natural fuel, is formed from the decomposed vegetation in the surrounding marshland over time. The peated Islay whisky has layers of flavor components. The first impression is a combination of hot smoke, cool ocean breeze, and green bogs; this is followed by a second layer made of fresh oolong tea, licorice, and yuzu skins; finally, a hidden layer of raspberry sorbet and lemongrass appears. When mixed with ingredients that have neutral flavors, Islay whisky's character shines through as a fresh addition to baked goods. On other occasions, its aroma transforms into something amazing in the presence of tropical fruits. The use of passionfruit, mango, and melon with Islay whisky creates a memorable culinary experience. The bright peatiness amplifies the pungent sweet smells of ripened fruits. When paired with dark chocolate, Islay whisky unveils a new dimension of flavors—roasted coffee beans, toasted pine nuts, and peat smoke. The brightness of Islay whisky transcends an ordinary dessert and turns it into a culinary masterpiece in paradise!

A toast to bakers and whiskey enthusiasts alike: May the discovery of baking with American rye and Islay Scotch make you appreciate these two heavenly elixirs even more and may the fruit of your labor bring enjoyment to your family and friends. Whiskey!

Sea Salt Caramel

Ingredients *(Yield: around 280 g/10 oz)*

150 g/5.3 oz granulated sugar
100 g/3.5 oz heavy cream
0.25 tsp sea salt (around 1 g/0.035 oz)
80 g/2.8 oz softened cream cheese
30 g/1.1 oz Islay Scotch whisky

Melt the sugar in a large saucepan over medium-low heat. Stir occasionally. In another saucepan, boil the cream and sea salt. Set aside.

Cook the sugar to a dark amber color, pour hot cream over the caramel and stir. Transfer the caramel to a large bowl.

When the caramel is warm to the touch, add the cream cheese and whiskey. Blend the mixture until it is smooth using a blender or mixer.

Cranberry Jam

Ingredients *(Yield: around 350 g/12.3 oz)*

150 g/5.3 oz granulated sugar
0.5 tsp pectin (around 1.5 g/0.053 oz)
200 g/7.1 oz cranberry puree
30 g/1.1 oz American rye whiskey
70 g/2.5 oz softened butter

Mix the sugar and pectin in a bowl and set aside.

Boil the cranberry puree in a saucepan. Add the sugar-pectin mixture into the pan, and then stir constantly. Cook the jam over low heat for about 10 minutes. Transfer the jam to a bowl.

Add whiskey and butter, and then mix well. Let cool before using.

Almond Paste

Ingredients *(Yield: around 220 g/7.8 oz)*

150 g/5.3 oz almond flour
50 g/1.8 oz granulated sugar
1 egg white (around 30 g/1.1 oz)
0.5 tsp almond extract (around 2.5 g/0.088 oz)

In a food processor, blend all ingredients into a paste. Reserve.

Banana Mash

COMPONENTS

Ingredients *(Yield: around 580 g/20 oz)*

150 g/5.3 oz almond flour
30 g/1.1 oz light brown sugar
1 tsp instant dry yeast (around 5 g/0.18 oz)
200 g/7.1 oz milk
30 g/1.1 oz American rye whiskey
2 bananas, broken into large pieces (around 200 g/7.1 oz)

Mix all ingredients in a large mixing bowl. Cover the bowl with plastic wrap. Allow the mash to ferment at room temperature overnight.

Serve the banana mash with cranberry jam (Page 7) in shot glasses if desired. Reserve the remaining mash for other baking needs.

Cranberry Macaroons

AMERICAN RYE

Ingredients *(Yield: about 24 cookies)*

100 g/3.5 oz almond flour
60 g/2.1 oz light brown sugar
2 egg whites (around 60 g/2.1 oz)
60 g/2.1 oz softened cream cheese
20 g/0.71 oz American rye whiskey
Cranberry jam (Page 7)
Powdered sugar for dusting

In a large mixing bowl, blend almond flour, sugar, egg whites, cream cheese, and whiskey using a blender or mixer.

Place the batter in a large pastry piping bag. Pipe the batter into 2.5-cm/1-in mounds on a baking pan lined with parchment paper. Bake the cookies at 177°C/350°F for about 20 minutes. Let cool completely.

Pipe or spread the cranberry jam in between two cookies to make sandwiches. Dust the macaroons with powdered sugar.

Banana Cookies

AMERICAN RYE

Ingredients *(Yield: about 30 cookies)*

150 g/5.3 oz almond flour
100 g/3.5 oz all-purpose flour
50 g/1.8 oz light brown sugar
1 egg (around 50 g/1.8 oz)
50 g/1.8 oz softened cream cheese
50 g/1.8 oz softened butter
30 g/1.1 oz American rye whiskey
1 banana, broken into pieces (around 100 g/3.5 oz)

In a large mixing bowl, combine all ingredients and mix well.

Spoon the dough into 2.5-cm/1-in mounds and place them on a baking pan lined with parchment paper. Bake the cookies at 185°C/365°F for about 20 minutes.

Banana Mash Dessert Glasses

Ingredients

Coin Cookies:
50 g/1.8 oz almond flour
50 g/1.8 oz cake flour
200 g/7.1 oz almond paste (Page 7)
3 eggs (around 150 g/5.3 oz)
30 g/1.1 oz American rye whiskey
15 g/0.53 oz softened butter
50 g/1.8 oz cranberry jam (Page 7)

Finishing:
Heavy cream
Light brown sugar
Banana mash (Page 8)

Coin Cookies:
In a large mixing bowl, blend all ingredients for the coin cookies into a batter using a mixer or blender. Allow the batter to rest for about an hour.

Transfer the batter into a large pastry piping bag. Pipe the batter into 1.3-cm/0.5-in mounds on a baking pan lined with parchment paper. Bake the cookies at 185°C/365°F for about 15 minutes until well browned around the edges. Let cool completely.

Finishing:
Whisk the cream with sugar. Arrange coin cookies, whipped cream, and a small amount of banana mash in glasses. Serve.

Breakfast Pancakes

Ingredients *(Yield: about 24 pancakes)*

50 g/1.8 oz almond flour
60 g/2.1 oz light brown sugar
100 g/3.5 oz all-purpose flour
150 g/5.3 oz banana mash (Page 8)
3 eggs (around 150 g/5.3 oz)
50 g/1.8 oz heavy cream

In a mixing bowl, combine all ingredients and mix well. Cover the bowl with plastic wrap. Allow the batter to ferment at room temperature overnight.

Heat a sauté pan over medium heat; add a small amount of vegetable oil. Pour about two spoons full of batter into the hot pan. Cook the pancake until both sides are golden brown. Finish the remaining batter in batches.

Banana Scones

Ingredients *(Yield: 12 scones)*

150 g/5.3 oz almond flour
150 g/5.3 oz all-purpose flour
300 g/10.6 oz banana mash (Page 8)
100 g/3.5 oz softened butter
Light brown sugar for the topping

In a mixing bowl, combine the flours, banana mash, and butter. Mix well. Cover the bowl with plastic wrap. Allow the dough to rise at room temperature overnight.

Divide the dough into twelve equal portions and place them on a baking pan lined with parchment paper. Allow the dough to rest for about 15 minutes. Sprinkle light brown sugar on top of the scones. Bake the scones at 191°C/375°F for about 25 minutes until golden.

AMERICAN RYE

Banana Mini-Loaves

AMERICAN RYE

Ingredients *(Yield: about 12 mini-loaves)*

200 g/7.1 oz all-purpose flour
200 g/7.1 oz almond flour
300 g/10.6 oz banana mash (Page 8)
4 eggs (around 200 g/7.1 oz)
60 g/2.1 oz heavy cream

In a mixing bowl. Combine all ingredients and mix well. Cover the bowl with plastic wrap. Allow the batter to ferment at room temperature overnight.

Grease a mini-loaf pan with butter. Fill each loaf cavity to about 70% full. Allow the batter to rest for about 20 minutes. Bake the loaves at 185°C/365°F for about 20 minutes.

Almond Bread Rolls

AMERICAN RYE

Ingredients *(Yield: about 12 bread rolls)*

150 g/5.3 oz all-purpose flour
1 tsp instant dry yeast (around 5 g/0.18 oz)
100 g/3.5 oz almond paste (Page 7)
100 g/3.5 oz milk
5 eggs (around 250 g/8.8 oz)
30 g/1.1 oz melted butter
30 g/1.1 oz American rye whiskey

In a mixing bowl, combine all ingredients and mix well. Cover the bowl with plastic wrap. Allow the batter to ferment at room temperature overnight.

Grease a mini-popover pan with butter; fill each cavity with the batter to about 75% full. Bake the rolls at 191°C/375°F for about 25 minutes until golden.

Rustic Raisin Loaves

Ingredients *(Yield: 7 loaves)*

200 g/7.1 oz all-purpose flour
100 g/3.5 oz almond flour
20 g/0.71 oz light brown sugar
2 tsp instant dry yeast (around 10 g/0.35 oz)
100 g/3.5 oz milk
2 eggs (around 100 g/3.5 oz)
30 g/1.1 oz softened cream cheese
30 g/1.1 oz American rye whiskey
50 g/1.8 oz raisins

In a mixing bowl, combine all ingredients and mix well. Cover the bowl with plastic wrap. Allow the dough to rise at room temperature overnight.

Divide the dough into seven loaves and place the loaves on a baking pan lined with parchment paper. Allow the loaves to rest for about 10 minutes. Bake the bread at 185°C/365°F for about 25 minutes.

Pumpkin Bread Rolls

26

AMERICAN RYE

Ingredients *(Yield: about 12 bread rolls)*

150 g/5.3 oz almond flour
50 g/1.8 oz all-purpose flour
30 g/1.1 oz light brown sugar
1 tsp instant dry yeast (around 5 g/0.18 oz)
3 eggs (around 150 g/5.3 oz)
200 g/7.1 oz pumpkin puree
30 g/1.1 oz American rye whiskey
30 g/1.1 oz softened butter
50 g/1.8 oz golden raisins

In a mixing bowl, combine all ingredients and mix well. Cover the bowl with plastic wrap. Allow the batter to ferment at room temperature overnight.

Grease a mini-popover pan with butter; stir the batter gently. Fill each cavity with the batter to about 60% full. Allow the batter to rest for about 15 minutes. Bake the rolls at 185°C/365°F for about 30 minutes until golden.

Puff Pastry Almond Tarts

AMERICAN RYE

Ingredients *(Yield: 7 individual tarts)*

150 g/5.3 oz almond paste (Page 7)
150 g/5.3 oz sour cream
3 eggs (around 150 g/5.3 oz)
50 g/1.8 oz American rye whiskey
200 g/7.1 oz puff pastry dough
Cranberry jam (Page 7)

In a mixing bowl, combine the almond paste, sour cream, eggs, and whiskey. Mix well. Chill the filling for about an hour.

Roll out the puff pastry dough to about 0.33-cm/0.13-in thick. Dock the dough with a fork. Cut the dough into seven large pieces, and then line the cavities of a large muffin pan with the dough. Bake the tart crusts at 191°C/375°F for about 30 minutes until golden.

Fill the baked tart crusts with chilled filling. Add a small amount of cranberry jam into the filling. Continue to bake the tarts for another 10 minutes.

Bread Pudding

AMERICAN RYE

Ingredients

200 g/7.1 oz almond paste (Page 7)
150 g/5.3 oz heavy cream
50 g/1.8 oz American rye whiskey
3 eggs (around 150 g/5.3 oz)
450 g/1 lb stale banana bread and/or scones, broken into large pieces

In a mixing bowl, combine all ingredients except for the bread pieces. Mix well. Carefully fold bread pieces into the batter. Pour the pudding mixture into a 23-cm/9-in pie dish. Bake the pie at 185°C/365°F for about 30 minutes.

WHISKEY BAKE

Peach Custard Pie

Ingredients

Crust:
150 g/5.3 oz almond flour
30 g/1.1 oz light brown sugar
60 g/2.1 oz softened butter
30 g/1.1 oz American rye whiskey

Filling:
400 g/14.1 oz peaches, cut into 1.3-cm/0.5-in pieces
20 g/0.71 oz almond flour
100 g/3.5 oz heavy cream
200 g/7.1 oz milk
200 g/7.1 oz softened cream cheese
4 eggs (around 200 g/7.1 oz)
30 g/1.1 oz American rye whiskey
30 g/1.1 oz light brown sugar

In a mixing bowl, mix all ingredients for the crust into a dough without over kneading. Press the dough by hand into the base of a 23-cm/9-in pie dish.

For the filling, toss the peaches with 20 g/0.71 oz of almond flour and set aside. In another large mixing bowl, mix the rest of the ingredients for the filling. Fill the pie crust with the peaches, and then pour the filling mixture on top of the peaches.

Bake the pie at 177°C/350°F for about 35 minutes. Let cool completely. Allow the pie to set in the refrigerator overnight. Serve chilled.

Cherry Cake Ring

Ingredients

Whiskey Cherries:
20 pitted red cherries
150 g/5.3 oz American rye whiskey

Cake Batter:
100 g/3.5 oz almond flour
100 g/3.5 oz all-purpose flour
60 g/2.1 oz light brown sugar
1 tsp baking soda (around 5 g/0.18 oz)
100 g/3.5 oz milk
3 eggs (around 150 g/5.3 oz)
60 g/2.1 oz softened butter
60 g/2.1 oz softened cream cheese
60 g/2.1 oz American rye whiskey

Cherry Whiskey Icing:
100 g/3.5 oz softened cream cheese
100 g/3.5 oz heavy cream
15 g/0.53 oz cherry soaking whiskey
30 g/1.1 oz light brown sugar

In a covered container, soak the cherries in whiskey for a few hours.

In a mixing bowl, blend all ingredients for the cake batter with a mixer or blender. Grease a 20-cm/8-in tube pan with butter. Pour the batter into the pan. Place nine whiskey cherries in the batter. Bake the cake at 185°C/365°F for about 30 minutes. Let cool completely.

Turn the cake bottom side up onto a serving plate. Whisk the ingredients for the cherry whiskey icing to soft peaks in a bowl. Moisten the cake with the remaining cherry soaking whiskey. Spoon the icing over the cake, and then arrange the remaining whiskey cherries on top of the cake.

Chocolate Peat

ISLAY SCOTCH

Ingredients *(Yield: about 30 pieces)*

200 g/7.1 oz high-quality bittersweet chocolate in small pieces
50 g/1.8 oz high-quality milk chocolate in small pieces
30 g/1.1 oz Islay Scotch whisky
30 g/1.1 oz softened cream cheese
Cocoa powder

Place the chocolate pieces in a bowl; melt the chocolates in a microwave oven. Stir the chocolate pieces every 30 seconds until they are completely melted. Add the whisky and stir again, and finally stir in the cream cheese.

Place the chocolate ganache between two pieces of parchment paper. Flatten the ganache to about 1-cm/0.4-in thick. Allow the ganache to set completely at room temperature overnight.

Cut the ganache into pieces, and then cover the pieces with cocoa powder.

Macaroons

ISLAY SCOTCH

Ingredients *(Yield: about 30 cookies)*

200 g/7.1 oz almond paste (Page 7)
100 g/3.5 oz almond flour
2 eggs (around 100 g/3.5 oz)
100 g/3.5 oz softened cream cheese
30 g/1.1 oz Islay Scotch whisky
Raw sugar crystals for the topping

In a large mixing bowl, blend all ingredients except for the topping sugar crystals using a blender or mixer.

Place the batter in a large pastry piping bag. Pipe the batter into 3.8-cm/1.5-in mounds on a baking pan lined with parchment paper.

Top the cookies with raw sugar crystals. Bake the cookies at 191°C/375°F for about 25 minutes.

Double-Baked Cookies

Ingredients *(Yield: about 30 cookies)*

100 g/3.5 oz cake flour
200 g/7.1 oz almond paste (Page 7)
2 eggs (around 100 g/3.5 oz)
100 g/3.5 oz heavy cream
20 g/0.71 oz Islay Scotch whisky

In a mixing bowl, blend all ingredients with a blender or mixer. Grease four cavities of a mini-loaf pan with butter. Fill the cavities with the batter to about 70% full. Bake the loaves at 185°C/365°F for 35 minutes. Let cool completely,

Cut the loaves into slices and place them on a baking pan lined with parchment paper. Bake the cookie slices again for another 10 to 15 minutes until golden. Dip the cookies in Islay whisky if desired.

Cranberry-Almond Gems

ISLAY SCOTCH

Ingredients *(Yield: about 40 cookies)*

250 g/8.8 oz almond flour
50 g/1.8 oz light brown sugar
3 egg whites (around 100 g/3.5 oz)
60 g/2.1 oz softened cream cheese
30 g/1.1 oz Islay Scotch whisky
Cranberry jam (Page 7)

In a mixing bowl, blend all ingredients except for the cranberry jam with a blender or mixer.

Place the batter in a large pastry piping bag. Pipe the batter into 2.5-cm/1-in mounds on a baking pan lined with parchment paper. Add a small amount of cranberry jam on top of each cookie. Bake the cookies at 185°C/365°F for about 20 minutes.

Rustic Shortbread

Ingredients *(Yield: about 30 cookies)*

75 g/2.6 oz almond flour
150 g/5.3 oz all-purpose flour
30 g/1.1 oz light brown sugar
1 egg (around 50 g/1.8 oz)
50 g/1.8 oz softened butter
50 g/1.8 oz softened cream cheese
15 g/0.53 oz Islay Scotch whisky

In a large mixing bowl, combine all ingredients and mix well.

Spoon the dough into 2.5-cm/1-in mounds and place them on a baking pan lined with parchment paper. Flatten the cookies slightly. Bake the cookies at 185°C/365°F for about 25 minutes.

Dessert Cake Spoons

ISLAY SCOTCH

Ingredients *(Yield: about 12 spoon-cakes)*

100 g/3.5 oz almond flour
100 g/3.5 oz light brown sugar
3 egg whites (around 100 g/3.5 oz)
100 g/3.5 oz softened cream cheese
30 g/1.1 oz Islay Scotch whisky
Cranberry jam (Page 7) and/or sea salt caramel (Page 6)

In a mixing bowl, blend all ingredients except for the jam and/or caramel using a blender or mixer.

Fill soup spoons with the cake batter. Add a small amount of jam and/or caramel in the center of each spoon.

Cook each spoon-cake in a microwave oven for about 20 seconds.

Almond Cakes

ISLAY SCOTCH

Ingredients *(Yield: about 12 cakes)*

100 g/3.5 oz almond flour
4 eggs (around 200 g/7.1 oz)
60 g/2.1 oz heavy cream
60 g/2.1 oz light brown sugar
60 g/2.1 oz vegetable oil
60 g/2.1 oz softened cream cheese
30 g/1.1 oz Islay Scotch whisky
Light brown sugar for the topping

In a large mixing bowl, blend all ingredients except for the topping sugar using a blender or mixer.

Grease a mini-muffin pan with butter. Pour the cake batter into each cavity to about 70% full. Bake the cakes at 185°C/365°F for about 15 minutes. Sprinkle light brown sugar on top to finish.

Chocolate Cake Corks

ISLAY SCOTCH

Ingredients *(Yield: about 12 cakes)*

Cake Batter:
50 g/1.8 oz dark chocolate in small pieces
50 g/1.8 oz butter
150 g/5.3 oz almond flour
250 g/8.8 oz all-purpose flour
30 g/1.1 oz cocoa powder
50 g/1.8 oz light brown sugar
0.5 Tbsp baking powder (around 7.5 g/0.26 oz)
0.5 tsp baking soda (around 2.5 g/0.088 oz)
250 g/8.8 oz milk
3 eggs (around 150 g/5.3 oz)
100 g/3.5 oz softened cream cheese
1 tsp grated fresh ginger (around 5 g/0.18 oz)
50 g/1.8 oz honey
50 g/1.8 oz Islay Scotch whisky

Whiskey Topping:
80 g/2.8 oz softened cream cheese
40 g/1.4 oz Islay Scotch whisky
20 g/0.71 oz light brown sugar

Melt the chocolate and butter. Set aside. Mix the remaining ingredients for the cake batter in a mixing bowl. Add the reserved chocolate and butter. Mix well. Let the batter rest for about an hour.

Grease a mini-popover pan with butter. Fill each cavity with the batter to about 80% full. Combine all ingredients for the whiskey topping, and then add the mixture on top of the cake batter. Bake the cakes at 191°C/375°F for about 25 minutes.

WHISKEY BAKE

Islay Bread Rolls

Ingredients *(Yield: 12 bread rolls)*

Batter:
200 g/7.1 oz all-purpose flour
300 g/10.6 oz almond flour
60 g/2.1 oz light brown sugar
2 tsp instant dry yeast (around 10 g/0.35 oz)
250 g/8.8 oz milk
4 eggs (around 200 g/7.1 oz)
60 g/2.1 oz Islay Scotch whisky

Filling:
Softened butter
Light brown sugar

Mix all ingredients for the batter in a large mixing bowl. Cover the bowl with plastic wrap. Allow the batter to ferment at room temperature overnight.

Grease a mini-popover pan with butter. Fill the cavities with the batter to about 30% full. Add a small amount of butter and light brown sugar, and then fill the cavities to about 70% full with more batter. Allow the batter to rest for about 10 minutes. Bake at 191°C/375°F for 15 minutes until golden.

Islay Loaves

ISLAY SCOTCH

Ingredients *(Yield: about 7 loaves)*

200 g/7.1 oz all-purpose flour
100 g/3.5 oz almond flour
20 g/0.71 oz light brown sugar
2 tsp instant dry yeast (around 10 g/0.35 oz)
100 g/3.5 oz milk
50 g/1.8 oz softened butter
50 g/1.8 oz softened cream cheese
50 g/1.8 oz Islay Scotch whisky

Mix all ingredients in a large mixing bowl. Cover the bowl with plastic wrap. Allow the dough to ferment at room temperature overnight.

Divide the dough into seven loaves, and then place the loaves on a baking pan lined with parchment paper. Allow the loaves to rest for about 10 minutes. Bake the bread at 185°C/365°F for about 25 minutes.

Raspberry Cake Puddings

Ingredients *(Yield: about 4 individual servings)*

Batter:
150 g/5.3 oz almond paste (Page 7)
4 eggs (around 200 g/7.1 oz)
30 g/1.1 oz Islay Scotch whisky
30 g/1.1 oz heavy cream

Raspberry Sauce:
50 g/1.8 oz raspberry puree
15 g/0.53 oz almond paste (Page 7)
15 g/0.53 oz Islay Scotch whisky
15 g/0.53 oz heavy cream

Blend all ingredients for the batter using a blender or mixer. Pour about 25% of the batter onto a baking pan lined with parchment paper. Bake the batter at 191°C/375°F for about 25 minutes until the cake sheet is well browned. Repeat to make a second batch. Allow the cake sheets to cool. Break the cake sheets into large pieces and reserve.

Meanwhile, combine all ingredients for the raspberry sauce. Set aside. In ramekins or individual ceramic baking dishes, layer the cake pieces, the remaining cake batter, and the raspberry sauce alternately. Finish the puddings in a 191°C/375°F oven for about 2 minutes. Serve warm.

Apple and Peach Pie

Ingredients

Pie Crust:
100 g/3.5 oz almond flour
100 g/3.5 oz all-purpose flour
50 g/1.8 oz light brown sugar
50 g/1.8 oz heavy cream
30 g/1.1 oz softened butter
30 g/1.1 oz Islay Scotch whisky

Filling:
2 large green apples and 2 large peaches, peeled and cut into large chunks (about 800 g/28.2 oz)
30 g/1.1 oz light brown sugar
30 g/1.1 oz almond flour
30 g/1.1 oz Islay Scotch whisky

Mix all ingredients for the pie crust into a dough without over kneading the dough. Take about 70% of the dough and press it into a 23-cm/9-in pie pan by hand. Bake the crust at 185°C/365°F for about 10 minutes.

Mix all ingredients for the filling in a large mixing bowl. Pour the filling into the pre-baked pie crust. Break the remaining pie dough into penny-sized pieces and scatter the dough on top of the filling. Bake at 185°C/365°F for about 30 minutes.

Melon-Passionfruit Cake Ring

Ingredients

Cake Dough:
100 g/3.5 oz almond flour
100 g/3.5 oz all-purpose flour
1 tsp instant dry yeast (around 5 g/0.18 oz)
30 g/1.1 oz light brown sugar
100 g/3.5 oz milk
3 eggs (around 150 g/5.3 oz)
30 g/1.1 oz Islay Scotch whisky
30 g/1.1 oz softened cream cheese

Melon Cocktail:
300 g/10.6 oz melons, cut into cubes
50 g/1.8 oz passionfruit puree
30 g/1.1 oz Islay Scotch whisky
30 g/1.1 oz light brown sugar

Whiskey Melon Cream:
120 g/4.2 oz heavy cream
30 g/1.1 oz softened cream cheese
30 g/1.1 oz melon cocktail liquid

Combine all ingredients for the cake dough. Mix well. Cover the bowl with plastic wrap. Allow the dough to rise at room temperature overnight.

In a covered container, combine all ingredients for the melon cocktail. Allow the melons to soak for a few hours.

Grease a 20-cm/8-in tube pan with butter. Fill the pan with the cake dough. Let the dough rest for another hour. Bake the cake at 185°C/365°F for 20 to 25 minutes. Let cool completely.

Turn the cake bottom side up; moisten the cake with the melon cocktail liquid. Whisk the ingredients for the whiskey melon cream to soft peaks. Spoon the cream over the cake. Arrange the melon pieces on top of the cream.

Mango Loaf Cake

Ingredients

Mango Cocktail:
1 large mango, cut into cubes (around 200 g/7.1 oz)
50 g/1.8 oz Islay Scotch whisky

Cake Batter:
150 g/5.3 oz cake flour
100 g/3.5 oz almond flour
2 tsp baking powder (around 10 g/0.35 oz)
4 eggs (around 200 g/7.1 oz)
50 g/1.8 oz softened butter
50 g/1.8 oz Islay Scotch whisky
50 g/1.8 oz milk
50 g/1.8 oz light brown sugar
1 banana, cut into pieces (around 100 g/3.5 oz)
Sea salt caramel (optional, Page 6)

Mango Whiskey Icing:
100 g/3.5 oz heavy cream
100 g/3.5 oz softened cream cheese
30 g/1.1 oz light brown sugar
30 g/1.1 oz mango cocktail liquid

In a covered container, combine the mango cubes with whiskey; soak the mango cubes overnight.

In a large bowl, mix all ingredients for the cake batter except for the caramel. Grease a 20-cm/8-in loaf pan with butter; pour the batter into the pan. Add the caramel on top of the batter if desired. Bake the cake at 185°C/365°F for about 35 to 40 minutes. Let cool completely.

Using a blender or mixer to blend all ingredients for the mango whiskey icing. Moisten the cake with the mango cocktail liquid. Spoon the icing on top of the cake, and then arrange the mango cubes on top.

Rye Americano

60 ml/2 oz American rye whiskey
15 ml/0.5 oz amaretto liqueur
Lemon

In a double old-fashioned glass, pour the rye whiskey and amaretto liqueur over ice. Stir well. Garnish the cocktail with a slice of lemon.

Islay Beer

180 ml/6 oz ginger ale
7.5 ml/0.25 oz Islay Scotch whisky
Lemon

In a beer mug, pour the ginger ale and Islay Scotch whisky over ice. Squeeze a few drops of lemon juice over the top. Stir well. Garnish the drink with a slice of lemon.

COCKTAILS

Islay Sunset

45 ml/1.5 oz Islay Scotch whisky
30 ml/1 oz Triple Sec
7.5 ml/0.25 oz passionfruit puree
Grenadine

In a cocktail shaker, shake the first three ingredients with ice. Strain the mixture into a chilled martini glass. Finish the cocktail by adding a dash of grenadine.

www.ingramcontent.com/pod-product-compliance
Lightning Source LLC
Chambersburg PA
CBHW061225070526
44584CB00029B/3989